On Political Economy

by

Jean Jacques Rousseau

www.books.com.co

First Printing March 2016
Printed in the United States of America.
10 9 8 7 6 5 4 3 2 1

If this is a work of fiction, it is not meant to depict, portray or represent any particular real persons. All the characters, incidents and dialogues are the products of the author's imagination and are not to be construed as real. Any references or similarities to actual events, entities, real people, living or dead, or to real locales are intended to give the novel a sense of reality. Any similarity in other names, characters, entities, places and incidents is entirely coincidental.

LG Classics
New York, New York
www.books.com.co

A DISCOURSE ON POLITICAL ECONOMY

Jean Jacques Rousseau

THE word Economy, or OEconomy, is derived from oikos, a house, and nomos, law, and meant originally only the wise and legitimate government of the house for the common good of the whole family. The meaning of the term was then extended to the government of that great family, the State. To distinguish these two senses of the word, the latter is called general or political economy, and the former domestic or particular economy. The first only is discussed in the present discourse. Even if there were as close an analogy as many authors maintain between the State and the family, it would not follow that the rules of conduct proper for one of these societies would be also proper for the other. They differ too much in extent to be regulated in the same manner; and there will always be a great difference between domestic government, in which a father can see everything for himself, and civil government, where the chief sees hardly anything save through the eyes of others. To put both on an equality in this respect, the talents, strength, and all the faculties of the father would have to increase in proportion to the size of his family, and the soul of a powerful monarch would have to be, to that of an ordinary man, as the extent of his empire is to that of a private person's estate. But how could the government of the State be like that of the family, when the basis on which they rest is so different? The father being physically stronger than his children, his paternal authority, as long as they need his protection, may be reasonably said to be established by nature.

But in the great family, all the members of which are naturally equal, the political authority, being purely arbitrary as far as its institution is concerned, can be founded only on conventions, and the Magistrate can have no authority over the rest, except by virtue of the laws. The duties of a father are dictated to him by natural feelings, and in a manner that seldom allows him to neglect them. For rulers there is no such principle, and they are really obliged to the people only by what they themselves have promised to do, and the people have therefore a right to require of them. Another more important difference is that since the children have nothing but what they receive from their father, it is plain that all the rights of property belong to him, or emanate from him; but quite the opposite is the case in the great family, where the general administration is established only to secure individual property, which is antecedent to it.

The principal object of the work of the whole house is to preserve and increase the patrimony of the father, in order that he may be able some day to distribute it among his children without impoverishing them; whereas the wealth of the exchequer is only a means, often ill understood, of keeping the individuals in peace and plenty. In a word, the little family is destined to be extinguished, and to resolve itself some day into several families of a similar nature; but the great family, being constituted to endure for ever in the same condition, need not, like the small one, increase for the purpose of multiplying, but need only maintain itself; and it can easily be proved that any increase does it more harm than good. In the family, it is clear, for several reasons which lie in its very nature, that the father ought to command. In the first place, the authority ought not to be equally divided between father and mother; the government must be single, and in every division of opinion there must be one preponderant voice to decide.

Secondly, however lightly we may regard the disadvantages peculiar to women, yet, as they necessarily occasion intervals of inaction, this is a sufficient reason for excluding them from this supreme authority: for when the balance is perfectly even, a straw is enough to turn the scale. Besides, the husband ought to be able to superintend his wife's conduct, because it is of importance for him to be assured that the children, whom he is obliged to acknowledge and maintain, belong to no one but himself.

Thirdly, children should be obedient to their father, at first of necessity, and afterwards from gratitude: after having had their wants satisfied by him during one half of their lives, they ought to consecrate the other half to providing for his. Fourthly, servants owe him their services in exchange for the provision he makes for them, though they may break off the bargain as soon as it ceases to suit them. I say nothing here of slavery, because it is contrary to nature, and cannot be authorised by any right or law. There is nothing of all this in political society, in which the chief is so far from having any natural interest in the happiness of the individuals, that it is not uncommon for him to seek his own in their misery. If the magistracy is hereditary, a community of men is often governed by a child. If it be elective, innumerable inconveniences arise from such election; while in both cases all the advantages of paternity are lost. If you have but a single ruler, you lie at the discretion of a master who has no reason to love you: and if you have several, you must bear at once their tyranny and their divisions.

In a word, abuses are inevitable and their consequences fatal in every society where the public interest and the laws have no natural force, and are perpetually attacked by personal interest and the passions of the ruler and the members. Although the functions of the father of a family and those of the chief magistrate ought to make for the same object, they must do so in such different ways, and their duty and rights are so essentially distinct, that we cannot confound them without forming very false ideas about the fundamental laws of society, and falling into errors which are fatal to mankind. In fact, if the voice of nature is the best counsellor to which a father can listen in the discharge of his duty, for the Magistrate it is a false guide, which continually prevents him from performing his, and leads him on sooner or later to the ruin of himself and of the State, if he is not restrained by the most sublime virtue. The only precaution necessary for the father of a family is to guard himself against depravity, and prevent his natural inclinations from being corrupted; whereas it is these themselves which corrupt the Magistrate. In order to act aright, the first has only to consult his heart; the other becomes a traitor the moment he listens to his. Even his own reason should be suspect to him, nor should he follow any rule other than the public reason, which is the law. Thus nature has made a multitude of good fathers of families; but it is doubtful whether, from the very beginning of the world, human wisdom has made ten men capable of governing their peers. From all that has just been said, it follows that public economy, which is my subject, has been rightly distinguished from private economy, and that, the State having nothing in common with the family except the obligations which their heads lie under of making both of them happy, the same rules of conduct cannot apply to both. I have considered these few lines enough to overthrow the detestable system which Sir Robert Filmer has endeavoured to establish in his Patriarcha; a work to which two celebrated writers have done too much honour in writing books to refute it.

Moreover, this error is of very long standing; for Aristotle himself thought proper to combat it with arguments which may be found in the first book of his Politics. I must here ask my readers to distinguish also between public economy, which is my subject and which I call government, and the supreme authority, which I call Sovereignty; a distinction which consists in the fact that the latter has the right of legislation, and in certain cases binds the body of the nation itself, while the former has only the right of execution, and is binding only on individuals. I shall take the liberty of making use of a very common, and in some respects inaccurate, comparison, which will serve to illustrate my meaning. The body politic, taken individually, may be considered as an organised, living body, resembling that of man. The sovereign power represents the head; the laws and customs are the brain, the source of the nerves and seat of the understanding, will and senses, of which the Judges and Magistrates are the organs: commerce, industry, and agriculture are the mouth and stomach which prepare the common subsistence; the public income is the blood, which a prudent economy, in performing the functions of the heart, causes to distribute through the whole body nutriment and life: the citizens are the body and the members, which make the machine live, move and work; and no part of this machine can be damaged without the painful impression being at once conveyed to the brain, if the animal is in a state of health. The life of both bodies is the self common to the whole, the reciprocal sensibility and internal correspondence of all the parts. Where this communication ceases, where the formal unity disappears, and the contiguous parts belong to one another only by juxtaposition, the man is dead, or the State is dissolved. The body politic, therefore, is also a moral being possessed of a will; and this general will, which tends always to the preservation and welfare of the whole and of every part, and is the source of the laws, constitutes for all the members of the State, in their relations to one another and to it, the rule of what is just or unjust: a truth which shows, by the way, how idly some writers have treated as theft the subtlety prescribed to children at Sparta for obtaining their frugal repasts, as if everything ordained by the law were not lawful. It is important to observe that this rule of justice, though certain with regard to all citizens, may be defective with regard to foreigners.

The reason is clear. The will of the State, though general in relation to its own members, is no longer so in relation to other States and their members, but becomes, for them, a particular and individual will, which has its rule of justice in the law of nature. This, however, enters equally into the principle here laid down; for in such a case, the great city of the world becomes the body politic, whose general will is always the law of nature, and of which the different States and peoples are individual members. From these distinctions, applied to each political society and its members, are derived the most certain and universal rules, by which we can judge whether a government is good or bad, and in general of the morality of all human actions. Every political society is composed of other smaller societies of different kinds, each of which has its interests and its rules of conduct: but those societies which everybody perceives, because they have an external and authorised form, are not the only ones that actually exist in the State: all individuals who are united by a common interest compose as many others, either transitory or permanent, whose influence is none the less real because it is less apparent, and the proper observation of whose various relations is the true knowledge of public morals and manners. The influence of all these tacit or formal associations causes, by the influence of their will, as many different modifications of the public will. The will of these particular societies has always two relations; for the members of the association, it is a general will; for the great society, it is a particular will; and it is often right with regard to the first object, and wrong as to the second. An individual may be a devout priest, a brave soldier, or a zealous senator, and yet a bad citizen.

A particular resolution may be advantageous to the smaller community, but pernicious to the greater. It is true that particular societies being always subordinate to the general society in preference to others, the duty of a citizen takes precedence of that of a senator, and a man's duty of that of a citizen: but unhappily personal interest is always found in inverse ratio to duty, and increases in proportion as the association grows narrower, and the engagement less sacred; which irrefragably proves that the most general will is always the most just also, and that the voice of the people is in fact the voice of God. It does not follow that the public decisions are always equitable; they may possibly, for reasons which I have given, not be so when they have to do with foreigners.

Thus it is not impossible that a Republic, though in itself well governed, should enter upon an unjust war. Nor is it less possible for the Council of a Democracy to pass unjust decrees, and condemn the innocent; but this never happens unless the people is seduced by private interests, which the credit or eloquence of some clever persons substitutes for those of the State: in which case the general will will be one thing, and the result of the public deliberation another. This is not contradicted by the case of the Athenian Democracy; for Athens was in fact not a Democracy, but a very tyrannical Aristocracy, governed by philosophers and orators. Carefully determine what happens in every public deliberation, and it will be seen that the general will is always for the common good; but very often there is a secret division, a tacit confederacy, which, for particular ends, causes the natural disposition of the assembly to be set at nought. In such a case the body of society is really divided into other bodies, the members of which acquire a general will, which is good and just with respect to these new bodies, but unjust and bad with regard to the whole, from which each is thus dismembered. We see then how easy it is, by the help of these principles, to explain those apparent contradictions, which are noticed in the conduct of many persons who are scrupulously honest in some respects, and cheats and scoundrels in others, who trample under foot the most sacred duties, and yet are faithful to the death to engagements that are often illegitimate.

Thus the most depraved of men always pay some sort of homage to public faith; and even robbers, who are the enemies of virtue in the great society, pay some respect to the shadow of it in their secret caves. In establishing the general will as the first principle of public economy, and the fundamental rule of government, I have not thought it necessary to inquire seriously whether the Magistrates belong to the people, or the people to the Magistrates; or whether in public affairs the good of the State should be taken into account, or only that of its rulers. That question indeed has long been decided one way in theory, and another in practice; and in general it would be ridiculous to expect that those who are in fact masters will prefer any other interest to their own. It would not be improper, therefore, further to distinguish public economy as popular or tyrannical. The former is that of every State, in which there reigns between the people and the rulers unity of interest and will: the latter will necessarily exist wherever the government and the people have different interests, and, consequently, opposing wills. The rules of the latter are written at length in the archives of history, and in the satires of Machiavelli. The rules of the former are found only in the writings of those philosophers who venture to proclaim the rights of humanity.

I. The first and most important rule of legitimate or popular government, that is to say, of government whose object is the good of the people, is therefore, as I have observed, to follow in everything the general will. But to follow this will it is necessary to know it, and above all to distinguish it from the particular will, beginning with one's self: this distinction is always very difficult to make, and only the most sublime virtue can afford sufficient illumination for it. As, in order to will, it is necessary to be free, a difficulty no less great than the former arises — that of preserving at once the public liberty and the authority of government. Look into the motives which have induced men, once united by their common needs in a general society, to unite themselves still more intimately by means of civil societies: you will find no other motive than that of assuring the property, life and liberty of each member by the protection of all.

But can men be forced to defend the liberty of any one among them, without trespassing on that of others? And how can they provide for the public needs, without alienating the individual property of those who are forced to contribute to them? With whatever sophistry all this may be covered over, it is certain that if any constraint can be laid on my will, I am no longer free, and that I am no longer master of my own property, if any one else can lay a hand on it. This difficulty, which would have seemed insurmountable, has been removed, like the first, by the most sublime of all human institutions, or rather by a divine inspiration, which teaches mankind to imitate here below the unchangeable decrees of the Deity. By what inconceivable art has a means been found of making men free by making them subject; of using in the service of the State the properties, the persons and even the lives of all its members, without constraining and without consulting them; of confining their will by their own admission; of overcoming their refusal by that consent, and forcing them to punish themselves, when they act against their own will?

How can it be that all should obey, yet nobody take upon him to command, and that all should serve, and yet have no masters, but be the more free, as, in apparent subjection, each loses no part of his liberty but what might be hurtful to that of another? These wonders are the work of law. It is to law alone that men owe justice and liberty. It is this salutary organ of the will of all which establishes, in civil right, the natural equality between men. It is this celestial voice which dictates to each citizen the precepts of public reason, and teaches him to act according to the rules of his own judgment, and not to behave inconsistently with himself. It is with this voice alone that political rulers should speak when they command; for no sooner does one man, setting aside the law, claim to subject another to his private will, than he departs from the state of civil society, and confronts him face to face in the pure state of nature, in which obedience is prescribed solely by necessity.

The most pressing interest of the ruler, and even his most indispensable duty, therefore, is to watch over the observation of the laws of which he is the minister, and on which his whole authority is founded. At the same time, if he exacts the observance of them from others, he is the more strongly bound to observe them himself, since he enjoys all their favour. For his example is of such force, that even if the people were willing to permit him to release himself from the yoke of the law, he ought to be cautious in availing himself of so dangerous a prerogative, which others might soon claim to usurp in their turn, and often use to his prejudice. At bottom, as all social engagements are mutual in nature, it is impossible for any one to set himself above the law, without renouncing its advantages; for nobody is bound by any obligation to one who claims that he is under no obligations to others. For this reason no exemption from the law will ever be granted, on any ground whatsoever, in a well-regulated government. Those citizens who have deserved well of their country ought to be rewarded with honours, but never with privileges: for the Republic is at the eve of its fall, when any one can think it fine not to obey the laws. If the nobility or the soldiery should ever adopt such a maxim, all would be lost beyond redemption.

The power of the laws depends still more on their own wisdom than on the severity of their administrators, and the public will derives its greatest weight from the reason which has dictated it. Hence Plato looked upon it as a very necessary precaution to place at the head of all edicts a preamble, setting forth their justice and utility. In fact, the first of all laws is to respect the laws: the severity of penalties is only a vain resource, invented by little minds in order to substitute terror for that respect which they have no means of obtaining.

It has constantly been observed that in those countries where legal punishments are most severe, they are also most frequent; so that the cruelty of such punishments is a proof only of the multitude of criminals, and, punishing everything with equal severity, induces those who are guilty to commit crimes, in order to escape being punished for their faults. But though the government be not master of the law, it is much to be its guarantor, and to possess a thousand means of inspiring the love of it. In this alone the talent of reigning consists. With force in one's hands, there is no art required to make the whole world tremble, nor indeed much to gain men's hearts; for experience has long since taught the people to give its rulers great credit for all the evil they abstain from doing it, and to adore them if they do not absolutely hate it. A fool, if he be obeyed, may punish crimes as well as another: but the true statesman is he who knows how to prevent them: it is over the wills, even more than the actions, of his subjects that his honourable rule is extended. If he could secure that every one should act aright, he would no longer have anything to do; and the masterpiece of his labours would be to be able to remain unemployed.

It is certain, at least, that the greatest talent a ruler can possess is to disguise his power, in order to render it less odious, and to conduct the State so peaceably as to make it seem to have no need of conductors. I conclude, therefore, that, as the first duty of the legislator is to make the laws conformable to the general will, the first rule of public economy is that the administration of justice should be conformable to the laws. It will even be enough to prevent the State from being ill governed, that the Legislator shall have provided, as he should, for every need of place, climate, soil, custom, neighbourhood, and all the rest of the relations peculiar to the people he had to institute. Not but what there still remains an infinity of details of administration and economy, which are left to the wisdom of the government: but there are two infallible rules for its good conduct on these occasions; one is, that the spirit of the law ought to decide in every particular case that could not be foreseen; the other is that the general will, the source and supplement of all laws, should be consulted wherever they fail.

But how, I shall be asked, can the general will be known in cases in which it has not expressed itself? Must the whole nation be assembled together at every unforeseen event? Certainly not. It ought the less to be assembled, because it is by no means certain that its decision would be the expression of the general will; besides, the method would be impractible in a great people, and is hardly ever necessary where the government is well-intentioned: for the rulers well know that the general will is always on the side which is most favourable to the public interest, that is to say, most equitable; so that it is needful only to act justly, to be certain of following the general will. When this is flouted too openly, it makes itself felt, in spite of the formidable restraint of the public authority. I shall cite the nearest possible examples that may be followed in such cases. In China, it is the constant maxim of the Prince to decide against his officers, in every dispute that arises between them and the people. If bread be too dear in any province, the Intendant of that province is thrown into prison. If there be an insurrection in another, the Governor is dismissed, and every Mandarin answers with his head for all the mischief that happens in his department. Not that these affairs do not subsequently undergo a regular examination; but long experience has caused the judgment to be thus anticipated.

There is seldom any injustice to be repaired; in the meantime, the Emperor, being satisfied that public outcry does not arise without cause, always discovers, through the seditious clamours which he punishes, just grievances to redress. It is a great thing to preserve the rule of peace and order through all the parts of the Republic; it is a great thing that the State should be tranquil, and the law respected: but if nothing more is done, there will be in all this more appearance than reality; for that government which confines itself to mere obedience will find difficulty in getting itself obeyed. If it is good to know how to deal with men as they are, it is much better to make them what there is need that they should be. The most absolute authority is that which penetrates into a man's inmost being, and concerns itself no less with his will than with his actions. It is certain that all peoples become in the long run what the government makes them; warriors, citizens, men, when it so pleases: or merely populace and rabble, when it chooses to make them so. Hence every prince who despises his subjects, dishonours himself, in confessing that he does not know how to make them worthy of respect. Make men, therefore, if you would command men: if you would have them obedient to the laws, make them love the laws, and then they will need only to know what is their duty to do it. This was the great art of ancient governments, in those distant times when philosophers gave laws to men, and made use of their authority only to render them wise and happy. Thence arose the numerous sumptuary laws, the many regulations of morals, and all the public rules of conduct which were admitted or rejected with the greatest care. Even tyrants did not forget this important part of administration, but took as great pains to corrupt the morals of their slaves, as Magistrates took to correct those of their fellow-citizens. But our modern governments, which imagine they have done everything when they have raised money, conceive that it is unnecessary and even impossible to go a step further.

II. The second essential rule of public economy is no less important than the first. If you would have the general will accomplished, bring all the particular wills into conformity with it; in other words, as virtue is nothing more than this conformity of the particular wills with the general will, establish the reign of virtue. If our politicians were less blinded by their ambition, they would see how impossible it is for any establishment whatever to act in the spirit of its institution, unless it is guided in accordance with the law of duty;

they would feel that the greatest support of public authority lies in the hearts of the citizens, and that nothing can take the place of morality in the maintenance of government. It is not only upright men who know how to administer the laws; but at bottom only good men know how to obey them. The man who once gets the better of remorse, will not shrink before punishments which are less severe, and less lasting, and from which there is at least the hope of escaping: whatever precautions are taken, those who only require impunity in order to do wrong will not fail to find means of eluding the law, and avoiding its penalties. In this case, as all particular interests unite against the general interest, which is no longer that of any individual, public vices have a greater effect in enervating the laws than the laws in the repression of such vices: so that the corruption of the people and of their rulers will at length extend to the government, however wise it may be.

The worst of all abuses is to pay an apparent obedience to the laws, only in order actually to break them with security. For in this case the best laws soon become the most pernicious; and it would be a hundred times better that they should not exist. In such a situation, it is vain to add edicts to edicts and regulations to regulations. Everything serves only to introduce new abuses, without correcting the old. The more laws are multiplied, the more they are despised, and all the new officials appointed to supervise them are only so many more people to break them, and either to share the plunder with their predecessors, or to plunder apart on their own. The reward of virtue soon becomes that of robbery; the vilest of men rise to the greatest credit; the greater they are the more despicable they become; their infamy appears even in their dignities, and their very honours dishonour them. If they buy the influence of the leaders or the protection of women, it is only that they may sell justice, duty, and the State in their turn: in the meantime, the people, feeling that its vices are not the first cause of its misfortunes, murmurs and complains that all its misfortunes come solely from those whom it pays to protect it from such things. It is under these circumstances that the voice of duty no longer speaks in men's hearts, and their rulers are obliged to substitute the cry of terror, or the lure of an apparent interest, of which they subsequently trick their creatures. In this situation they are compelled to have recourse to all the petty and despicable shifts which they call rules of State and mysteries of the cabinet.

All the vigour that is left in the government is used by its members in ruining and supplanting one another, while the public business is neglected, or is transacted only as personal interest requires and directs. In short, the whole art of those great politicians lies in so mesmerising those they stand in need of, that each may think he is labouring for his own interest in working for theirs: I say theirs on the false supposition that it is the real interest of rulers to annihilate a people in order to make it subject, and to ruin their own property in order to secure their possession of it. But when the citizens love their duty, and the guardians of the public authority sincerely apply themselves to the fostering of that love by their own example and assiduity, every difficulty vanishes; and government becomes so easy that it needs none of that art of darkness, whose blackness is its only mystery. Those enterprising spirits, so dangerous and so much admired, all those great ministers, whose glory is inseparable from the miseries of the people, are no longer regretted: public morality supplies what is wanting in the genius of the rulers; and the more virtue reigns, the less need there is for talent. Even ambition is better served by duty than by usurpation: when the people is convinced that its rulers are labouring only for its happiness, its deference saves them the trouble of labouring to strengthen their power: and history shows us, in a thousand cases, that the authority of one who is beloved over those whom he loves is a hundred times more absolute than all the tyranny of usurpers. This does not mean that the government ought to be afraid to make use of its power, but that it ought to make use of it only in a lawful manner. We find in history a thousand examples of pusillanimous or ambitious rulers, who were ruined by their slackness or their pride; not one who suffered for having been strictly just. But we ought not to confound negligence with moderation, or clemency with weakness. To be just, it is necessary to be severe; to permit vice, when one has the right and the power to suppress it, is to be oneself vicious. It is not enough to say to the citizens, be good; they must be taught to be so; and even example, which is in this respect the first lesson, is not the sole means to be employed; patriotism is the most efficacious: for, as I have said already, every man is virtuous when his particular will is in all things conformable to the general will, and we voluntarily will what is willed by those whom we love.

It appears that the feeling of humanity evaporates and grows feeble in embracing all mankind, and that we cannot be affected by the calamities of Tartary or Japan, in the same manner as we are by those of European nations. It is necessary in some degree to confine and limit our interest and compassion in order to make it active. Now, as this sentiment can be useful only to those with whom we have to live, it is proper that our humanity should confine itself to our fellow-citizens, and should receive a new force because we are in the habit of seeing them, and by reason of the common interest which unites them. It is certain that the greatest miracles of virtue have been produced by patriotism: this fine and lively feeling, which gives to the force of self-love all the beauty of virtue, lends it an energy which, without disfiguring it, makes it the most heroic of all passions. This it is that produces so many immortal actions, the glory of which dazzles our feeble eyes; and so many great men, whose old-world virtues pass for fables now that patriotism is made mock of. This is not surprising; the transports of susceptible hearts appear altogether fanciful to any one who has never felt them; and the love of one's country, which is a hundred times more lively and delightful than the love of a mistress, cannot be conceived except by experiencing it. But it is easy to perceive in every heart that is warmed by it, in all the actions it inspires, a glowing and sublime ardour which does not attend the purest virtue, when separated from it. Contrast Socrates even with Cato; the one was the greater philosopher, the other more of the citizen. Athens was already ruined in the time of Socrates, and he had no other country

than the world at large. Cato had the cause of his country
always at heart; he lived for it alone, and could not bear to
outlive it. The virtue of Socrates was that of the wisest of
men; but, compared with Caesar and Pompey, Cato seems a
God among mortals. Socrates instructed a few individuals,
opposed the Sophists, and died for truth: but Cato defended
his country, its liberty and its laws, against the conquerors
of the world, and at length departed from the earth, when he
had no longer a country to serve. A worthy pupil of Socrates
would be the most virtuous of his contemporaries; but a worthy follower of Cato would be one of the greatest. The virtue
of the former would be his happiness; the latter would seek
his happiness in that of all. We should be taught by the one,
and led by the other; and this alone is enough to determine
which to prefer: for no people has ever been made into a nation of philosophers, but it is not impossible to make a people
happy. Do we wish men to be virtuous?

Then let us begin by making them love their country: but
how can they love it, if their country be nothing more to them
than to strangers, and afford them nothing but what it can
refuse nobody? It would be still worse, if they did not enjoy
even the privilege of social security, and if their lives, liber-
ties and property lay at the mercy of persons in power, without their being permitted, or it being possible for them, to
get relief from the laws. For in that case, being subjected to
the duties of the state of civil society, without enjoying even
the common privileges of the state of nature, and without
being able to use their strength in their own defence, they
would be in the worst condition in which freemen could possibly find themselves, and the word country would mean for
them something merely odious and ridiculous. It must not be
imagined that a man can break or lose an arm, without the
pain being conveyed to his head: nor is it any more credible
that the general will should consent that any one member of
the State, whoever he might be, should wound or destroy another, than it is that the fingers of a man in his senses should
wilfully scratch his eyes out. The security of individuals is
so intimately connected with the public confederation that,
apart from the regard that must be paid to human weakness,

that convention would in point of right be dissolved, if in the State a single citizen who might have been relieved were allowed to perish, or if one were wrongfully confined in prison, or if in one case an obviously unjust sentence were given. For the fundamental conventions being broken, it is impossible to conceive of any right or interest that could retain the people in the social union; unless they were restrained by force, which alone causes the dissolution of the state of civil society. In fact, does not the undertaking entered into by the whole body of the nation bind it to provide for the security of the least of its members with as much care as for that of all the rest?

Is the welfare of a single citizen any less the common cause than that of the whole State? It may be said that it is good that one should perish for all. I am ready to admire such a saying when it comes from the lips of a virtuous and worthy patriot, voluntarily and dutifully sacrificing himself for the good of his country: but if we are to understand by it, that it is lawful for the government to sacrifice an innocent man for the good of the multitude, I look upon it as one of the most execrable rules tyranny ever invented, the greatest falsehood that can be advanced, the most dangerous admission that can be made, and a direct contradiction of the fundamental laws of society. So little is it the case that any one person ought to perish for all, that all have pledged their lives and properties for the defence of each, in order that the weakness of individuals may always be protected by the strength of the public, and each member by the whole State.

Suppose we take from the whole people one individual after another, and then press the advocates of this rule to explain more exactly what they mean by the body of the State, and we shall see that it will at length be reduced to a small number of persons, who are not the people, but the officers of the people, and who, having bound themselves by personal oath to perish for the welfare of the people, would thence infer that the people is to perish for their own. Need we look for examples of the protection which the State owes to its members, and the respect it owes to their persons? It is only among the most illustrious and courageous nations that they are to be found; it is only among free peoples that the dignity of man is realised. It is well known into what perplexity the whole republic of Sparta was thrown, when the question of punishing a guilty citizen arose. In Macedon, the life of a man was a matter of such importance, that Alexander the Great, at the height of his glory, would not have dared to put a Macedonian criminal to death in cold blood, till the accused had appeared to make his defence before his fellow-citizens, and had been condemned by them. But the Romans distinguished themselves above all other peoples by the regard which their government paid to the individual, and by its scrupulous attention to the preservation of the inviolable rights of all the members of the State.

Nothing was so sacred among them as the life of a citizen; and no less than an assembly of the whole people was needed to condemn one. Not even the Senate, nor the Consuls, in all their majesty, possessed the right; but the crime and punishment of a citizen were regarded as a public calamity among the most powerful people in the world. So hard indeed did it seem to shed blood for any crime whatsoever, that by the Lex Porcia, the penalty of death was commuted into that of banishment for all those who were willing to survive the loss of so great a country. Everything both at Rome, and in the Roman armies, breathed that love of fellow-citizens one for another, and that respect for the Roman name, which raised the courage and inspired the virtue of every one who had the honour to bear it. The cap of a citizen delivered from slavery, the civic crown of him who had saved the life of another, were looked upon with the greatest pleasure amid the pomp of their triumphs; and it is remarkable that among the crowns which were bestowed in honour of splendid actions in war, the civic crown and that of the triumphant general alone were of laurel, all the others being merely of gold. It was thus that Rome was virtuous and became the mistress of the world. Ambitious rulers! A herdsman governs his dogs and cattle, and yet is only the meanest of mankind. If it be a fine thing to command, it is when those who obey us are capable of doing us honour. Show respect, therefore, to your fellow-citizens, and you will render yourselves worthy of respect; show respect to liberty, and your power will increase daily. Never exceed your rights, and they will soon become unlimited. Let our country then show itself the common mother of her citizens; let the advantages they enjoy in their country endear it to them; let the government leave them enough share in the public administration to make them feel that they are at home; and let the laws be in their eyes only the guarantees of the common liberty. These rights, great as they are, belong to all men: but without seeming to attack them directly, the ill-will of rulers may in fact easily reduce their effect to nothing. The law, which they thus abuse, serves the powerful at once as a weapon of offence, and as a shield against the weak; and the pretext of the public good is always the most dangerous scourge of the people. What is most necessary, and perhaps most difficult, in government, is rigid integrity in doing strict justice to all, and above all in protecting the poor against the tyranny of the rich.

The greatest evil has already come about, when there are poor men to be defended, and rich men to be restrained. It is on the middle classes alone that the whole force of the law is exerted; they are equally powerless against the treasures of the rich and the penury of the poor. The first mocks them, the second escapes them. The one breaks the meshes, the other passes through them. It is therefore one of the most important functions of government to prevent extreme inequality of fortunes; not by taking away wealth from its possessors, but by depriving all men of means to accumulate it; not by building hospitals for the poor, but by securing the citizens from becoming poor. The unequal distribution of inhabitants over the territory, when men are crowded together in one place, while other places are depopulated; the encouragement of the arts that minister to luxury and of purely industrial arts at the expense of useful and laborious crafts; the sacrifice of agriculture to commerce; the necessitation of the tax-farmer by the mal-administration of the funds of the State; and in short, venality pushed to such an extreme that even public esteem is reckoned at a cash value, and virtue rated at a market price: these are the most obvious causes

of opulence and of poverty, of public interest, of mutual ha-
tred among citizens, of indifference to the common cause, of
the corruption of the people, and of the weakening of all the
springs of government. Such are the evils, which are with
difficulty cured when they make themselves felt, but which
a wise administration ought to prevent, if it is to maintain,
along with good morals, respect for the laws, patriotism, and
the influence of the general will. But all these precautions
will be inadequate, unless rulers go still more to the root of
the matter. I conclude this part of public economy where I
ought to have begun it. There can be no patriotism without
liberty, no liberty without virtue, no virtue without citizens;
create citizens, and you have everything you need; without
them, you will have nothing but debased slaves, from the rulers of the State downwards.

To form citizens is not the work of a day; and in order
to have men it is necessary to educate them when they are
children. It will be said, perhaps, that whoever has men to
govern, ought not to seek, beyond their nature, a perfection
of which they are incapable; that he ought not to desire to
destroy their passions; and that the execution of such an at-
tempt is no more desirable than it is possible. I will agree,
further, that a man without passions would certainly be a
bad citizen; but it must be agreed also that, if men are not
taught not to love some things, it is impossible to teach them
to love one object more than another — to prefer that which
is truly beautiful to that which is deformed. If, for example,
they were early accustomed to regard their individuality
only in its relation to the body of the State, and to be aware,
so to speak, of their own existence merely as a part of that of
the State, they might at length come to identify themselves
in some degree with this greater whole, to feel themselves
members of their country, and to love it with that exquisite
feeling which no isolated person has save for himself; to lift
up their spirits perpetually to this great object, and thus to
transform into a sublime virtue that dangerous disposition
which gives rise to all our vices. Not only does philosophy
demonstrate the possibility of giving feeling these new di-
rections; history furnishes us with a thousand striking ex-

amples. If they are so rare among us moderns, it is because nobody troubles himself whether citizens exist or not, and still less does anybody think of attending to the matter soon enough to make them. It is too late to change our natural inclinations, when they have taken their course, and egoism is confirmed by habit: it is too late to lead us out of ourselves when once the human Ego, concentrated in our hearts, has acquired that contemptible activity which absorbs all virtue and constitutes the life and being of little minds. How can patriotism germinate in the midst of so many other passions which smother it? And what can remain, for fellow-citizens, of a heart already divided between avarice, a mistress, and vanity?

From the first moment of life, men ought to begin learning to deserve to live; and, as at the instant of birth we partake of the rights of citizenship, that instant ought to be the beginning of the exercise of our duty. If there are laws for the age of maturity, there ought to be laws for infancy, teaching obedience to others: and as the reason of each man is not left to be the sole arbiter of his duties, government ought the less indiscriminately to abandon to the intelligence and prejudices of fathers the education of their children, as that education is of still greater importance to the State than to the fathers: for, according to the course of nature, the death of the father often deprives him of the final fruits of education; but his country sooner or later perceives its effects. Families dissolve, but the State remains.

Should the public authority, by taking the place of the father, and charging itself with that important function, acquire his rights by discharging his duties, he would have the less cause to complain, as he would only be changing his title, and would have in common, under the name of citizen, the same authority over his children, as he was exercising separately under the name of father, and would not be less obeyed when speaking in the name of the law, than when he spoke in that of nature. Public education, therefore, under regulations prescribed by the government, and under magistrates established by the Sovereign, is one of the fundamental rules of popular or legitimate government. If children are brought up in common in the bosom of equality; if they are imbued with the laws of the State and the precepts of the general will; if they are taught to respect these above all things; if they are surrounded by examples and objects which constantly remind them of the tender mother who nourishes them, of the love she bears them, of the inestimable benefits they receive from her, and of the return they owe her, we cannot doubt that they will learn to cherish one another mutually as brothers, to will nothing contrary to the will of society, to substitute the actions of men and citizens for the futile and vain babbling of sophists, and to become in time defenders and fathers of the country of which they will have been so long the children. I shall say nothing of the Magistrates destined to preside over such an education, which is certainly the most important business of the State.

It is easy to see that if such marks of public confidence were conferred on slight grounds, if this sublime function were not, for those who have worthily discharged all other offices, the reward of labour, the pleasant and honourable repose of old age, and the crown of all honours, the whole enterprise would be useless and the education void of success. For wherever the lesson is not supported by authority, and the precept by example, all instruction is fruitless; and virtue itself loses its credit in the mouth of one who does not practise it. But let illustrious warriors, bent under the weight of their laurels, preach courage: let upright Magistrates, grown white in the purple and on the bench teach justice. Such teachers as these would thus get themselves virtuous successors, and transmit from age to age, to generations to come, the experience and talents of rulers, the courage and virtue of citizens, and common emulation in all to live and die for their country.

I know of but three peoples which once practised public education, the Cretans, the Lacedemonians, and the ancient Persians: among all these it was attended with the greatest success, and indeed it did wonders among the two last. Since the world has been divided into nations too great to admit of being well governed, this method has been no longer practicable, and the reader will readily perceive other reasons why such a thing has never been attempted by any modern people. It is very remarkable that the Romans were able to dispense with it; but Rome was for five hundred years one continued miracle which the world cannot hope to see again.

The virtue of the Romans, engendered by their horror of tyranny and the crimes of tyrants, and by an innate patriotism, made all their houses so many schools of citizenship; while the unlimited power of fathers over their children made the individual authority so rigid that the father was more feared than the Magistrate, and was in his family tribunal both censor of morals and avenger of the laws. Thus a careful and well-intentioned government, vigilant incessantly to maintain or restore patriotism and morality among the people, provides beforehand against the evils which sooner or later result from the indifference of the citizens to the fate of the Republic, keeping within narrow bounds that personal interest which so isolates the individual that the State is enfeebled by his power, and has nothing to hope from his goodwill. Wherever men love their country, respect the laws, and live simply, little remains to be done in order to make them happy; and in public administration, where chance has less influence than in the lot of individuals, wisdom is so nearly allied to happiness, that the two objects are confounded.

III. It is not enough to have citizens and to protect them, it is also necessary to consider their subsistence. Provision for the public wants is an obvious inference from the general will, and the third essential duty of government. This duty is not, we should feel, to fill the granaries of individuals and thereby to grant them a dispensation from labour, but to keep plenty so within their reach that labour is always necessary and never useless for its acquisition. It extends also to everything regarding the management of the exchequer, and the expenses of public administration. Having thus treated of general economy with reference to the government of persons, we must now consider it with reference to the admin-

istration of property. This part presents no fewer difficulties
to solve, and contradictions to remove, than the preceding. It
is certain that the right of property is the most sacred of all
the rights of citizenship, and even more important in some
respects than liberty itself; either because it more nearly af-
fects the preservation of life, or because, property being more
easily usurped and more difficult to defend than life, the law
ought to pay a greater attention to what is most easily tak-
en away; or finally, because property is the true foundation
of civil society, and the real guarantee of the undertakings
of citizens: for if property were not answerable for personal
actions, nothing would be easier than to evade duties and
laugh at the laws.

On the other hand, it is no less certain that the maintenance of the State and the government involves costs and
outgoings; and as every one who agrees to the end must ac-
quiesce in the means, it follows that the members of a society ought to contribute from their property to its support.
Besides, it is difficult to secure the property of individuals on
one side, without attacking it on another; and it is impossible
that all the regulations which govern the order of succession,
will, contracts, &c. should not lay individuals under some
constraint as to the disposition of their goods, and should not
consequently restrict the right of property. But besides what
I have said above of the agreement between the authority of
law and the liberty of the citizen, there remains to be made,
with respect to the disposition of goods, an important observation which removes many difficulties. As Puffendorf has
shown, the right of property, by its very nature, does not extend beyond the life of the proprietor, and the moment a man
is dead his goods cease to belong to him. Thus, to prescribe
the conditions according to which he can dispose of them, is
in reality less to alter his right as it appears, than to extend
it in fact.

In general, although the institution of the laws which
regulate the power of individuals in the disposition of their
own goods belongs only to the Sovereign, the spirit of these
laws, which the government ought to follow in their applica-

tion, is that, from father to son, and from relation to relation, the goods of a family should go as little out of it and be as little alienated as possible. There is a sensible reason for this in favour of children, to whom the right of property would be quite useless, if the father left them nothing, and who besides, having often contributed by their labour to the acquisition of their father's wealth, are in their own right associates with him in his right of property. But another reason, more distant, though not less important, is that nothing is more fatal to morality and to the Republic than the continual shifting of rank and fortune among the citizens: such changes are both the proof and the source of a thousand disorders, and overturn and confound everything; for those who were brought up to one thing find themselves destined for another; and neither those who rise nor those who fall are able to assume the rules of conduct, or to possess themselves of the qualifications requisite for their new condition, still less to discharge the duties it entails.

I proceed to the object of public finance. If the people governed itself and there were no intermediary between the administration of the State and the citizens, they would have no more to do than to assess themselves occasionally, in proportion to the public needs and the abilities of individuals: and as they would all keep in sight the recovery and employment of such assessments, no fraud or abuse could slip into the management of them; the State would never be involved in debt, or the people over-burdened with taxes; or at least the knowledge of how the money would be used would be a consolation for the severity of the tax. But things cannot be carried on in this manner: on the contrary, however small any State may be, civil societies are always too populous to be under the immediate government of all their members. It is necessary that the public money should go through the hands of the rulers, all of whom have, besides the interests of the State, their own individual interests, which are not the last to be listened to. The people, on its side, perceiving rather the cupidity and ridiculous expenditure of its rulers than the public needs, murmurs at seeing itself stripped of necessaries to furnish others with superfluities; and when once these complaints have reached a certain degree of bitterness, the most upright administration will find it impossible to restore confidence. In such a case, voluntary contributions bring in nothing, and forced contributions are illegitimate. This cruel alternative of letting the State perish, or of violating the sacred right of property, which is its support, constitutes the great difficulty of just and prudent economy.

The first step which the founder of a republic ought to take after the establishment of laws, is to settle a sufficient fund for the maintenance of the Magistrates and other Officials, and for other public expenses. This fund, if it consist of money, is called ararium or fisc, and public demesne if it consist of lands. This, for obvious reasons, is much to be preferred. Whoever has reflected on this matter must be of the opinion of Bodin, who looks upon the public demesne as the most reputable and certain means of providing for the needs of the State. It is remarkable also that Romulus, in his division of lands, made it his first care to set apart a third for the use of the State. I confess it is not impossible for the produce of the demesne, if it be badly managed, to be reduced to nothing; but it is not of the essence of public demesnes to be badly administered.

Before any use is made of this fund, it should be assigned or accepted by an assembly of the people, or of the estates of the country, which should determine its future use. After this solemnity, which makes such funds inalienable, their very nature is, in a manner, changed, and the revenues become so sacred, that it is not only the most infamous theft, but actual treason, to misapply them or pervert them from the purpose for which they were destined. It reflects great dishonour on Rome that the integrity of Cato the censor was something so very remarkable, and that an Emperor, on rewarding the talents of a singer with a few crowns, thought it necessary to observe that the money came from his own private purse, and not from that of the State. But if we find few Galbas, where are we to look for a Cato? For when vice is no longer dishonourable, what chiefs will be so scrupulous as to abstain from touching the public revenues that are left to their discretion, and even not in time to impose on themselves, by pretending to confound their own expensive and scandalous dissipations with the glory of the State, and the means of extending their own authority with the means of augmenting its power? It is particularly in this delicate part of the administration that virtue is the only effective instrument, and that the integrity of the Magistrate is the only real check upon his avarice. Books and auditing of accounts, instead of exposing frauds, only conceal them; for prudence is never so ready to conceive new precautions as knavery is to elude them. Never mind, then, about account books and papers; place the management of finance in honest hands: that is the only way to get it faithfully conducted. When public funds are once established, the rulers of the State become of right the administrators of them: for this administration constitutes a part of government which is always essential, though not always equally so.

Its influence increases in proportion as that of other resources is diminished; and it may justly be said that a government has reached the last stage of corruption, when it has ceased to have sinews other than money. Now as every government constantly tends to become lax, this is enough to show why no State can subsist unless its revenues constantly increase. The first sense of the necessity of this increase is also the first sign of the internal disorder of the State; and the prudent administrator, in his endeavours to find means to provide for the present necessity, will neglect nothing to find out the distance cause of the new need; just as a mariner when he finds the water gaining on his vessel, does not neglect, while he is working the pumps, to discover and stop the leak. From this rule is deduced the most important rule in the administration of finance, which is, to take more pains to guard against needs than to increase revenues. For, whatever diligence be employed, the relief which only comes after, and more slowly than, the evil, always leaves some injury behind. While a remedy is being found for one evil, another is beginning to make itself felt, and even the remedies themselves produce new difficulties: so that at length the nation is involved in debt and the people oppressed, while the government loses its influence and can do very little with a great deal of money. I imagine it was owing to the recognition of this rule that such wonders were done by ancient governments, which did more with their parsimony than ours do with all their treasures; and perhaps from this comes the common use of the word economy, which means rather the prudent management of what one has than ways of getting what one has not. But apart from the public demesne, which is of service to the State in proportion to the uprightness of those who govern, any one sufficiently acquainted with the whole force of the general administration, especially when it confines itself to legitimate methods, would be astonished at the resources the rulers can make use of for guarding against public needs, without trespassing on the goods of individuals. As they are masters of the whole commerce of the State, nothing is easier for them than to direct it into such channels as to provide for every need, without appearing to interfere.

The distribution of provisions, money, and merchandise in just proportions, according to times and places, is the true secret of finance and the source of wealth, provided those who administer it have foresight enough to suffer a present apparent loss, in order really to obtain immense profits in the future. When we see a government paying bounties, instead of receiving duties, on the exportation of corn in time of plenty, and on its importation in time of scarcity, we must have such facts before our eyes if we are to be persuaded of their reality. We should hold such facts to be idle tales, if they had happened in ancient times. Let us suppose that, in order to prevent a scarcity in bad years, a proposal were made to establish public granaries; would not the maintenance of so useful an institution serve in most countries as an excuse for new taxes?

At Geneva, such granaries, established and kept up by a prudent administration, are a public resource in bad years, and the principal revenue of the State at all times. Alit et ditat is the inscription which stands, rightly and properly, on the front of the building. To set forth in this place the economic system of a good government, I have often turned my eyes to that of this Republic, rejoicing to find in my own country an example of that wisdom and happiness which I should be glad to see prevail in every other. If we ask how the needs of a State grow, we shall find they generally arise, like the wants of individuals, less from any real necessity than from the increase of useless desires, and that expenses are often augmented only to give a pretext for raising receipts: so that the State would sometimes gain by not being rich, and apparent wealth is in reality more burdensome than poverty itself would be. Rulers may indeed hope to keep the peoples in stricter dependence, by thus giving them with one hand what they take from them with the other; and this was in fact the policy of Joseph towards the Egyptians: but this political sophistry is the more fatal to the State, as the money never returns into the hands it went out of. Such principles only enrich the idle at the expense of the industrious.

A desire for conquest is one of the most evident and dangerous causes of this increase. This desire, occasioned often by a different species of ambition from that which it seems to proclaim, is not always what it appears to be, and has not so much, for its real motive, the apparent desire to aggrandise the Nation as a secret desire to increase the authority of the rulers at home, by increasing the number of troops, and by the diversion which the objects of war occasion in the minds of the citizens. It is at least certain, that no peoples are so oppressed and wretched as conquering nations, and that their successes only increase their misery. Did not history inform us of the fact, reason would suffice to tell us that, the greater a State grows, the heavier and more burdensome in proportion its expenses become: for every province has to furnish its share to the general expense of government, and besides has to be at the expense of its own administration, which is as great as if it were really independent. Add to this that great fortunes are always acquired in one place and spent in another. Production therefore soon ceases to balance consumption, and a whole country is impoverished merely to enrich a single town. Another source of the increase of public wants, which depends on the foregoing, is this. There may come a time when the citizens, no longer looking upon themselves as

interested in the common cause, will cease to be the defenders of their country, and the Magistrates will prefer the command of mercenaries to that of free-men; if for no other reason than that, when the time comes, they may use them to
reduce free-men to submission. Such was the state of Rome
towards the end of the Republic and under the Emperors: for
all the victories of the early Romans, like those of Alexander,
had been won by brave citizens, who were ready, at need, to
give their blood in the service of their country, but would never sell it. Only at the siege of Veii did the practice of paying
the Roman infantry begin. Marius, in the Jugurthine war,
dishonoured the legions by introducing freedmen, vagabonds
and other mercenaries. Tyrants, the enemies of the very people it was their duty to make happy, maintained regular
troops, apparently to withstand the foreigner, but really to
enslave their countrymen. To form such troops, it was necessary to take men from the land; the lack of their labour then
diminished the amount of provisions, and their maintenance
introduced those taxes which increased prices.

This first disorder gave rise to murmurs among the people; in order to suppress them, the number of troops had
to be increased, and consequently the misery of the people
also got worse; and the growing despair led to still further
increases in the cause in order to guard against its effects.
On the other hand, the mercenaries, whose merit we may
judge of by the price at which they sold themselves, proud of
their own meanness, and despising the laws that protected
them, as well as their fellows whose bread they ate, imagined
themselves more honoured in being Caesar's satellites than
in being defenders of Rome. As they were given over to blind
obedience, their swords were always at the throats of their
fellow-citizens, and they were prepared for general butchery
at the first sign. It would not be difficult to show that this
was one of the principal causes of the ruin of the Roman Empire. The invention of artillery and fortifications has forced
the princes of Europe, in modern times, to return to the use
of regular troops, in order to garrison their towns; but, however lawful their motives, it is to be feared the effect may be
no less fatal. There is no better reason now than formerly for

depopulating the country to form armies and garrisons, nor should the people be oppressed to support them; in a word, these dangerous establishments have increased of late years with such rapidity in this part of the world, that they evidently threaten to depopulate Europe, and sooner or later to ruin its inhabitants. Be this as it may, it ought to be seen that such institutions necessarily subvert the true economic system, which draws the principal revenue of the State from the public demesne, and leave only the troublesome resource of subsidies and imposts; with which it remains to deal. It should be remembered that the foundation of the social compact is property; and its first condition, that every one should be maintained in the peaceful possession of what belongs to him. It is true that, by the same treaty, every one binds himself, at least tacitly, to be assessed toward the public wants: but as this undertaking cannot prejudice the fundamental law, and presupposes that the need is clearly recognised by all who contribute to it, it is plain that such assessment, in order to be lawful, must be voluntary; it must depend, not indeed on a particular will, as if it were necessary to have the consent of each individual, and that he should give no more than just what he pleased, but on a general will, decided by vote of a majority, and on the basis of a proportional rating which leaves nothing arbitrary in the imposition of the tax.

That taxes cannot be legitimately established except by the consent of the people or its representatives, is a truth generally admitted by all philosophers and jurists of any repute on questions of public right, not even excepting Bodin. If any of them have laid down rules which seem to contradict this, their particular motives for doing so may easily be seen; and they introduce so many conditions and restrictions that the argument comes at bottom to the same thing: for whether the people has it in its power to refuse, or the Sovereign ought not to exact, is a matter of indifference with regard to right; and if the point in question concerns only power, it is useless to inquire whether it is legitimate or not. Contributions levied on the people are two kinds; real, levied on commodities, and personal, paid by the head. Both are called taxes or subsidies: when the people fixes the sum to be paid, it is called subsidy; but when it grants the product of an imposition, it is called a tax. We are told in The Spirit of the Laws that a capitation tax is most suited to slavery, and a real tax most in accordance with liberty. This would be incontestable, if the circumstances of every person were equal; for otherwise nothing can be more disproportionate than such a tax; and it is in the observations of exact proportions that the spirit of liberty consists. But if a tax by heads were exactly proportioned to the circumstances of individuals, as what is called the capitation tax in France might be, it would be the most equitable and consequently the most proper for freemen. These proportions appear at first very easy to note, because, being relative to each man's position in the world, their incidence is always public: but proper regard is seldom paid to all the elements that should enter into such a calculation, even apart from deception arising from avarice, fraud and self-interest. In the first place, we have to consider the relation of quantities, according to which, ceteris paribus, the person who has ten times the property of another man ought to pay ten times as much to the State.

Secondly, the relation of the use made, that is to say, the distinction between necessaries and superfluities. He who possesses only the common necessaries of life should pay nothing at all, while the tax on him who is in possession of superfluities may justly be extended to everything he has over and above mere necessaries. To this he will possibly object that, when his rank is taken into account, what may be superfluous to a man of inferior station is necessary for him. But this is false: for a grandee has two legs just like a cowherd, and, like him again, but one belly. Besides, these pretended necessaries are really so little necessary to his rank, that if he should renounce them on any worthy occasion, he would only be the more honoured. The populace would be ready to adore a Minister who went to Council on foot, because he had sold off his carriages to supply a pressing need of the State.

Lastly, to no man does the law prescribe magnificence; and propriety is no argument against right. A third relation, which is never taken into account, though it ought to be the chief consideration, is the advantage that every person derives from the social confederacy; for this provides a powerful protection for the immense possessions of the rich, and hardly leaves the poor man in quiet possession of the cottage he builds with his own hands. Are not all the advantages of society for the rich and powerful? Are not all lucrative posts in their hands? Are not all privileges and exemptions reserved for them alone? Is not the public authority always on their side? If man of eminence robs his creditors, or is guilty of other knaveries, is he not always assured of impunity? Are not the assaults, acts of violence, assassinations, and even murders committed by the great, matters that are hushed up in a few months, and of which nothing more is thought? But if a great man himself is robbed or insulted, the whole police force is immediately in motion, and woe even to innocent persons who chance to be suspected. If he has to pass through any dangerous road, the country is up in arms to escort him.

If the axle-tree of his chaise breaks, everybody flies to his assistance. If there is a noise at his door, he speaks but a word, and all is silent. If he is incommoded by the crowd, he waves his hand and every one makes way. If his coach is met on the road by a wagon, his servants are ready to beat the driver's brains out, and fifty honest pedestrians going quietly about their business had better be knocked on the head than an idle jackanapes be delayed in his coach. Yet all this respect costs him not a farthing: it is the rich man's right, and not what he buys with his wealth. How different is the case of the poor man! the more humanity owes him, the more society denies him. Every door is shut against him, even when he has a right to its being opened: and if ever he obtains justice, it is with much greater difficulty than others obtain favours. If the militia is to be raised or the highway to be mended, he is always given the preference; he always bears the burden which his richer neighbour has influence enough to get exempted from. On the least accident that happens to him, everybody avoids him: if his cart be overturned in the road, so far is he from receiving any assistance, that he is lucky if he does not get horse-whipped by the impudent lackeys of some young Duke; in a word, all gratuitous assistance is denied to the poor when they need it, just because they cannot pay for it. I look upon any poor man as totally undone, if he has the misfortune to have an honest heart, a fine daughter, and a powerful neighbour. Another no less important fact is that the losses of the poor are much harder to repair than those of the rich, and that the difficulty of acquisition is always greater in proportion as there is more need for it. "Nothing comes out of nothing," is as true of life as in physics: money is the seed of money, and the first guinea is sometimes more difficult to acquire than the second million. Add to this that what the poor pay is lost to them for ever, and remains in, or returns to, the hands of the rich: and as, to those who share in the government or to their dependents, the whole produce of the taxes must sooner or later pass, although they pay their share, these persons have always a sensible interest in increasing them. The terms of the social compact between these two estates of men may be summed up in a few words.

"You have need of me, because I am rich and you are poor. We will therefore come to an agreement. I will permit you to have the honour of serving me, on condition that you bestow on me the little you have left, in return for the pains I shall take to command you." Putting all these considerations carefully together, we shall find that, in order to levy taxes in a truly equitable and proportionate manner, the imposition ought not to be in simple ratio to the property of the contributors, but in compound ratio to the difference of their conditions and the superfluity of their possessions. This very important and difficult operation is daily made by numbers of honest clerks, who know their arithmetic; but a Plato or a Montesquieu would not venture to undertake it without the greatest diffidence, or without praying to Heaven for understanding and integrity. Another disadvantage of personal taxes is that they may be too much felt or raised with too great severity. This, however, does not prevent them from being frequently evaded; for it is much easier for persons to escape a tax than for their possessions. Of all impositions, that on land, or real taxation, has always been regarded as most advantageous in countries where more attention is paid to what the tax will produce, and to the certainty of recovering the product, than to securing the least discomfort for the people. It has been even maintained that it is necessary to burden the peasant in order to rouse him from indolence, and that he would never work if he had no taxes to pay. But in all countries experience confutes this ridiculous notion. In England and Holland the farmer pays very little, and in China nothing: yet these are the countries in which the land is best cultivated. On the other hand, in those countries where the husbandman is taxed in proportion to the produce of his lands, he leaves them uncultivated, or reaps just as much from them as suffices for bare subsistence. For to him who loses the fruit of his labour, it is some gain to do nothing. To lay a tax on industry is a very singular expedient for banishing idleness. Taxes on land or corn, especially when they are excessive, lead to two results so fatal in their effect that they cannot but depopulate and ruin, in the long run, all countries in which they are established. The first of these arises from the defective circulation of specie; for industry and commerce draw all the money from the country into the capitals: and as the tax destroys the proportion there might otherwise be between the needs of the husbandman and the price of his corn, money is always leaving and never returning. Thus the richer the city the poorer the country.

The product of the taxes passes from the hands of the Prince or his financial officers into those of artists and traders; and the husbandman, who receives only the smallest part of it, is at length exhausted by paying always the same, and receiving constantly less. How could a human body subsist if it had veins and no arteries, or if its arteries conveyed the blood only within four inches of the heart? Chardin tells us that in Persia the royal dues on commodities are paid in kind: this custom, which, Herodotus informs us, prevailed long ago in the same country down to the time of Darius, might prevent the evil of which I have been speaking. But unless intendants, directors, commissioners, and warehousemen in Persia are a different kind of people from what they

are elsewhere, I can hardly believe that the smallest part of
this produce ever reaches the king, or that the corn is not
spoilt in every granary, and the greater part of the warehous-
es not consumed by fire. The second evil effect arises from an
apparent advantage, which aggravates the evil before it can
be perceived. That is that corn is a commodity whose price
is not enhanced by taxes in the country producing it, and
which, in spite of its absolute necessity, may be diminished
in quantity without the price being increased. Hence, many
people die of hunger, although corn remains cheap, and the
husbandman bears the whole charge of a tax, for which he
cannot indemnify himself by the price of his corn.

It must be observed that we ought not to reason about a
land-tax in the same manner as about duties laid on various
kinds of merchandise; for the effect of such duties is to raise
the price, and they are paid by the buyers rather than the
sellers. For these duties, however heavy, are still voluntary,
and are paid by the merchant only in proportion to the quantity he buys; and as he buys only in proportion to his sale, he
himself gives the law its particular application; but the farmer who is obliged to pay his rent at stated times, whether he
sells or not, cannot wait till he can get his own price for his
commodity: even if he is not forced to sell for mere subsistence, he must sell to pay the taxes; so that it is frequently
the heaviness of the tax that keeps the price of corn low. It
is further to be noticed that the resources of commerce and
industry are so far from rendering the tax more supportable
through abundance of money, that they only render it more
burdensome. I shall not insist on what is very evident; i.e.,
that, although a greater or less quantity of money in a State
may give it the greater or less credit in the eye of the foreigner, it makes not the least difference to the real fortune of the
citizens, and does not make their condition any more or less
comfortable. But I must make these two important remarks:
first, unless a State possesses superfluous commodities, and
abundance of money results from foreign trade, only trading
cities are sensible of the abundance; while the peasant only
becomes relatively poorer. Secondly, as the price of everything is enhanced by the increase of money, taxes also must

be proportionately increased; so that the farmer will find himself still more burdened without having more resources. It ought to be observed that the tax on land is a real duty on the produce. It is universally agreed, however, that nothing is so dangerous as a tax on corn paid by the purchaser: but how comes it we do not see that it is a hundred times worse when the duty is paid by the cultivator himself? Is not this an attack on the substance of the State at its very source? Is it not the directest possible method of depopulating a country, and therefore in the end ruining it? For the worst kind of scarcity a nation can suffer from is lack of inhabitants.

Only the real statesman can rise, in imposing taxes, above the mere financial object: he alone can transform heavy burdens into useful regulations, and make the people even doubtful whether such establishments were not calculated rather for the good of the nation in general, than merely for the raising of money. Duties on the importation of foreign commodities, of which the natives are fond, without the country standing in need of them; on the exportation of those of the growth of the country which are not too plentiful, and which foreigners cannot do without: on the productions of frivolous and all too lucrative arts; on the importation of all pure luxuries; and in general on all objects of luxury; will answer the two-fold end in view. It is by such taxes, indeed, by which the poor are eased, and the burdens thrown on the rich, that it is possible to prevent the continual increase of inequality of fortune; the subjection of such a multitude of artisans and useless servants to the rich, the multiplication of idle persons in our cities, and the depopulation of the country-side. It is important that the value of any commodity and the duties laid on it should be so proportioned that the avarice of individuals may not be too strongly tempted to fraud by the greatness of the possible profit.

To make smuggling difficult, those commodities should be singled out which are hardest to conceal. All duties should be rather paid by the consumer of the commodity taxed than by him who sells it: as the quantity of duty he would be obliged to pay would lay him open to greater temptations, and afford him more opportunities for fraud. This is the constant custom in China, a country where the taxes are greater and yet better paid than in any other part of the world. There the merchant himself pays no duty; the buyer alone, without murmuring or sedition, meets the whole charge; for as the necessaries of life, such as rice and corn, are absolutely exempt from taxation, the common people is not oppressed, and the duty falls only on those who are well-to-do. Precautions against smuggling ought not to be dictated so much by the fear of it occurring, as by the attention which the government should pay to securing individuals from being seduced by illegitimate profits, which first make them bad citizens, and afterwards soon turn them into dishonest men. Heavy taxes should be laid on servants in livery, on equipages, rich furniture, fine clothes, on spacious courts and gardens, on public entertainments of all kinds, on useless professions, such as dancers, singers, players, and in a word, on all that multiplicity of objects of luxury, amusement and idleness, which strike the eyes of all, and can the less be hidden, as their whole purpose is to be seen, without which they would be useless.

We need be under no apprehension of the produce of these taxes being arbitrary, because they are laid on things not absolutely necessary. They must know but little of mankind who imagine that, after they have been once seduced by luxury, they can ever renounce it: they would a hundred times sooner renounce common necessaries, and had much rather die of hunger than of shame. The increase in their expense is only an additional reason for supporting them, when the vanity of appearing wealthy reaps its profit from the price of the thing and the charge of the tax. As long as there are rich people in the world, they will be desirous of distinguishing themselves from the poor, nor can the State devise a revenue less burdensome or more certain than what arises from this distinction. For the same reason, industry would have nothing to suffer from an economic system which increased the revenue, encouraged agriculture by relieving the husbandman, and insensibly tended to bring all fortunes nearer to that middle condition which constitutes the genuine strength of the State. These taxes might, I admit, bring certain fashionable articles of dress and amusement to an untimely end; but it would be only to substitute others, by which the artificer would gain, and the exchequer suffer no loss. In a word, suppose the spirit of government was constantly to tax only the superfluities of the rich, one of two things must happen: either the rich would convert their superfluous expenses into useful ones, which would redound to the profit of the State, and thus the imposition of taxes would have the effect of the best sumptuary laws, the expenses of the State would necessarily diminish with those of individuals, and the treasury would not receive so much less as it would gain by having less to pay; or, if the rich did not become less extravagant, the exchequer would have such resources in the product of taxes on their expenditure as would provide for the needs of the State. In the first case the treasury would be the richer by what it would save, from having the less to do with its money; and in the second, it would be enriched by the useless expenses of individuals.

We may add to all this a very important distinction in matters of political right, to which governments, constantly tenacious of doing everything for themselves, ought to pay great attention. It has been observed that personal taxes and duties on the necessaries of life, as they directly trespass on the right of property, and consequently on the true foundation of political society, are always liable to have dangerous results, if they are not established with the express consent of the people or its representatives. It is not the same with articles the use of which we can deny ourselves; for as the individual is under no absolute necessity to pay, his contribution may count as voluntary. The particular consent of each contributor then takes the place of the general consent of the whole people: for why should a people oppose the imposition of a tax which falls only on those who desire to pay it? It appears to me certain that everything, which is not proscribed by law, or contrary to morality, and yet may be prohibited by the government, may also be permitted on payment of a certain duty. Thus, for example, if the government may prohibit the use of coaches, it may certainly impose a tax on them; and this is a prudent and useful method of censuring their use without absolutely forbidding it. In this case, the tax may be regarded as a sort of fine, the product of which compensates for the abuse it punishes. It may perhaps be objected that those, whom Bodin calls impostors, i.e., those who impose or contrive the taxes, being in the class of the rich, will be far from sparing themselves to relieve the poor. But this is quite beside the point. If, in every nation, those to whom the Sovereign commits the government of the people, were, from their position, its enemies, it would not be worth while to inquire what they ought to do to make the people happy.

www.ingramcontent.com/pod-product-compliance
Lightning Source LLC
Chambersburg PA
CBHW070842310526
45793CB00011B/516